Original title:
Freedom from Routine

Copyright © 2024 Creative Arts Management OÜ
All rights reserved.

Author: Thor Castlebury
ISBN HARDBACK: 978-9916-88-402-7
ISBN PAPERBACK: 978-9916-88-403-4

The Odyssey of Everyday Wonder

In morning light the world awakes,
With whispered dreams and gentle shakes.
A cup of tea, the warmth it brings,
In simple moments, happiness sings.

The rustle of leaves, a breeze so light,
Children laughing, pure delight.
A stranger's smile, a glance exchanged,
In fleeting seconds, hearts are changed.

Starlit skies at dusky dawn,
The glow of dusk, a magic drawn.
City streets, a vibrant hue,
Each corner hides a tale or two.

In everyday life, a quest unfolds,
With wonders waiting, and joys untold.
Through every step, let hearts discover,
The beauty in the world, our everyday treasure.

The Colorful Burst of a New Dawn

A canvas bright, the day awakes,
With hues of orange, pink, and gold.
The sun ascends, a warm embrace,
As dreams of night begin to fold.

Birds take flight in morning's light,
Their songs of joy fill up the air.
Each ray that shines, a sweet delight,
Awakening hearts, casting care.

Straying Beyond Familiar Paths

Footsteps lead to places unknown,
Worn trails fade beneath the leaves.
Curiosity brightly shone,
In whispers, adventure weaves.

Turning corners, stretching views,
Every breath, a chance to grow.
In the wild, excitement brews,
Finding magic where winds blow.

Singing in the Silence of the Mundane

In quiet moments, life unfolds,
Amid the hum of daily grinds.
The simple joy, a heart of gold,
In hidden treasures, peace one finds.

Washing dishes, folding clothes,
A melody in every task.
With gentle rhythm, the spirit flows,
In life's small things, the joy we ask.

Stars in the Spaces Between

In twilight's hush, the cosmos gleams,
Stars sparkle in the velvet sky.
They whisper secrets through our dreams,
Inviting souls to reach and fly.

In gaps of light, stories collide,
Of ancient tales and future hopes.
Within each heartbeat, we confide,
Connected in this dance of scopes.

Laughter Beyond the Routines

In the morning sun, we gather bright,
Waking up early, embracing the light.
With giggles and grins, our hearts do ignite,
Chasing away shadows, it's pure delight.

Coffee brews strong, laughter fills the air,
Sharing our stories, we lighten our care.
The joy of togetherness, never a spare,
Moments like these, too precious to wear.

Fluttering Pages of Surprise

Whispers of wisdom, inked on each page,
Stories unfold, breaking every cage.
Characters dance, filled with joy and rage,
Each turn reveals a new, vibrant stage.

Under the moon, with a book in my hand,
Lost in the magic, where dreams can expand.
Fluttering pages, like grains of sand,
Each tale a treasure, vast and unplanned.

Constellations of New Adventures

Stars in the night, a map so divine,
Paths intertwined, our spirits align.
Chasing horizons, where dreams intertwine,
New adventures spark, in every design.

With each step forward, the world feels alive,
Uncharted journeys, where hopes can thrive.
Sailing the cosmos, we learn to dive,
Constellations glowing, together we strive.

Breaking the Rhythm

In the dance of life, a beat drifts away,
Shattering patterns that held us at bay.
Unconventional paths invite us to play,
New sounds emerging, come what may.

A burst of wild, a splash of bright hues,
Colors collide, creating new views.
Breaking the rhythm, we chase the muse,
In chaos, we find the freedom to choose.

Dancing Through Unfamiliar Streets

Under glowing signs we glide,
Footsteps light, hearts open wide.
Each corner holds a tale untold,
In the night, our spirits bold.

Lanterns flicker, shadows sway,
Lost in rhythm, we find our way.
With laughter echoing in the air,
Adventure waits, we have no care.

Strangers pass with knowing smiles,
Each moment cherished for a while.
In this dance, our souls unite,
Through the dark, we chase the light.

The Whisper of New Horizons

Beyond the clouds, the sun will rise,
A promise held in painted skies.
With each dawn, a chance to learn,
New horizons gently churn.

In our hearts, we weave a dream,
A future bright, a flowing stream.
With whispered hopes that glide on air,
We navigate without a care.

Winds will guide our steady flight,
Towards places bathed in light.
In the distance, wonders gleam,
Reality dances with the dream.

A Tapestry of Unwritten Days

Threads of time in colors bold,
Stories waiting to unfold.
Each moment a stitch in space,
A tapestry we each embrace.

With every dawn the canvas grows,
Painted paths where sunlight flows.
Unwritten days, a blank refrain,
A symphony of joy and pain.

Let us wander without a map,
In the unknown, we find the gap.
Every stroke bears meaning true,
The art of life in shades anew.

Embrace the Wild Unknown

In the wild where silence breathes,
Adventure waits beneath the leaves.
With open arms, we greet the day,
In nature's dance, we lose our way.

Mountains call with echoes strong,
Where the heart beats wild and long.
The untamed paths invite us near,
To face our fears without a tear.

Stars ignite the evening sky,
We'll chase the dreams that soar on high.
In the wild, we find our tone,
Together, brave, we're never alone.

Embracing the Unexpected Twilight

The sun dips low, a fiery glow,
Shadows stretch, the night's soft show.
In the stillness, whispers call,
Embrace the unknown, it beckons all.

Stars emerge in velvet skies,
Dreams take flight, as silence sighs.
Moments pause, we breathe in deep,
Awakening secrets we once did keep.

The Colorful Palette of Tomorrow

Brush strokes dance on canvas bright,
Colors clash, yet feel so right.
A tapestry of hopes and dreams,
In vivid hues, the future gleams.

Every shade a story told,
In bold expressions, dreams unfold.
With every hue, a chance to grow,
Painting paths we long to know.

Unraveled Threads of Comfort

In the fabric of everyday life,
Threads entwine, amidst the strife.
Each stitch carries memories dear,
Woven with love, drawing us near.

As we unravel, we find our way,
Discovering peace in the fray.
Soft whispers echo in our hearts,
A tapestry where healing starts.

The Symphony of New Beginnings

Dawn awakens with a gentle breeze,
New harmonies dance among the trees.
A symphony swells, inviting the day,
Every note a chance to play.

Melodies rise from the earth below,
An orchestra stirs, ready to grow.
With each heartbeat, a fresh refrain,
A song of hope, released from pain.

Unraveling Every Thread

In the weave of day, we find our ties,
Threads of laughter tangled in bright skies.
Each moment a stitch, each memory a hue,
Unraveling the tapestry, me and you.

The loom of fate spins tales we share,
With every heartbeat, a gentle prayer.
As colors fade, and shadows blend,
Unraveling threads, the journey won't end.

Breaking the Silence of the Usual

In the quiet corners where shadows dwell,
Breaking the silence, a silent bell.
Voices rise in a cacophony clear,
Challenging norms that we often fear.

The usual hum, a monotonous drone,
With every whisper, a truth to be known.
The cracks in the walls let the light seep,
Breaking the silence, awake from deep sleep.

The Pulse of Impromptu Dreams

Dreams unbidden, like stars in the night,
Flicker alive, a sudden delight.
In the chaos of moments, they twirl and spin,
The pulse of the heart, where visions begin.

With every heartbeat, they beckon us near,
Impromptu whispers that only we hear.
Dancing through shadows, in vibrant light,
The pulse of our dreams feels so perfectly right.

The Portraits of Random Joy

In a blink, we capture life's glee,
Portraits of moments, wild and free.
With every smile, a brushstroke of grace,
Random joy painted on each face.

Beneath the laughter, stories unfold,
Colors of happiness, bright and bold.
In the gallery of life, each memory glows,
The portraits we cherish, as love overflows.

A Canvas of the Unpredictable

Chaos paints the morning sky,
Brushstrokes dance in colors high.
Each hue tells a story new,
Of twists and turns we hold so true.

Wildflowers bloom in paths unknown,
Dreams take flight, seeds are sown.
The winds whisper secrets shared,
In the canvas, nothing is spared.

A spark ignites the fading light,
Trust the shadows, brace for flight.
Adventures carve their own design,
In unpredictable, we align.

With every step, the world unfolds,
Like ancient maps with tales retold.
In colors bold, we paint our fate,
A canvas true, it won't be late.

Swaying to the Rhythm of Instinct

In the silence, a heartbeat calls,
Whispers echo as twilight falls.
We sway beneath the silver moon,
Guided by an ancient tune.

The night unfurls its velvet wings,
In the dark, a freedom sings.
Movement flows, uncaged and free,
Dancing wild, just you and me.

Echoes of nature's sweet embrace,
In each step, we find our place.
Intuition leads the way tonight,
In rhythm's grasp, we feel the light.

Across the fields, where shadows blend,
Together, we sway, no end to bend.
With spirits high, the stars ignite,
We dance with life, pure and bright.

The Magic of Wandering Souls

Footsteps trace the paths of stars,
Searching for a home, perhaps Mars.
Wandering hearts, forever bold,
In the magic of stories told.

Through valleys deep and mountains high,
Lost in wonder, we drift and fly.
Each moment glimmers, a spark divine,
In the weave of fate, our souls entwine.

Mirrors of the universe shine,
In each stranger, a thread of time.
With every glance, a journey starts,
The magic flows through open hearts.

Together we roam, hand in hand,
Crafting dreams across the land.
In the dance of life, we find our role,
The magic lives in wandering souls.

Breaking Out of the Daily Grayscale

In the monotone of crowded streets,
Life's color fades, the heart retreats.
Yet beneath the gray, a spark remains,
Longing for freedom, breaking the chains.

Bright murals call from brick and stone,
Vibrant whispers in a monotone.
Brush against the dull with flair,
In every corner, possibility's air.

With each sunrise, a chance to bloom,
To shatter the silence, disperse the gloom.
A world in color, intense and bright,
Reclaims the canvas, ignites the light.

So let us dance in hues of bold,
Create with passion, let life unfold.
In breaking free, we find our way,
Out of the grayscale, into the day.

The Hues of Exploration

In valleys deep, where shadows play,
Colors blend in light of day.
Mountains rise, horizons wide,
Each step whispers stories inside.

Oceans stretch with waves of blue,
Secrets hidden, waiting for you.
Forests hum with life and sound,
In every corner, wonders found.

Skies ignite at dusk's embrace,
Stars appear, a cosmic race.
Journeys call, a beckoning tune,
Chasing dreams beneath the moon.

To wander free, to seek and find,
Unfolding tales, hearts intertwined.
The earth a palette, vast and grand,
With every footprint, magic spanned.

Repainting the Life Canvas

With brush in hand, we start anew,
Strokes of joy, in vibrant hue.
Past the sorrow, beyond the pain,
Each color brings a glimmering gain.

Layer by layer, we redefine,
Shades of hope within the line.
Every mishap, a splendid part,
Reshape the canvas, heal the heart.

Textures blend in wild delight,
Brushing shadows, seeking light.
Life's a masterpiece, ever true,
In every blend, the old and new.

Let us paint with laughter's sound,
In every drop, love can be found.
A world reborn, with dreams to chase,
Repainting life in our own grace.

A Symphony of Unplanned Moments

In every mishap, magic gleams,
Life's a dance of broken dreams.
A missed train or a turned street,
Leads to laughter, joy, and sweet.

Unexpected friends at dawn's break,
The warmth of smiles that fate makes.
Moments fleeting, yet they stay,
A symphony in shades of gray.

The wind whispers tales untold,
As seconds turn to tales of old.
With every twist, surprise unfolds,
A tune of life that never molds.

Embrace the chaos, feel the spark,
In unplanned days, adventures hark.
For in the wild, we come alive,
A symphony where hearts can thrive.

The Lure of the Unfamiliar

Beyond the horizon, call it fate,
Lies a world where dreams await.
The unknown beckons, a gentle plea,
In strange lands, we yearn to be free.

With every step on foreign ground,
New tastes and sights all around.
Glowing markets, bustling streets,
In every corner, adventure greets.

Voices blend in accents rare,
Stories woven with tender care.
In the unfamiliar, we find our song,
A symphony where we all belong.

Let curiosity pave the way,
To explore what words can't say.
For in the unfamiliar's embrace,
Lies the heart's most sacred place.

The Path Less Travelled

With whispers soft, it beckons me,
Through shadows dense and lights a-glee.
Each step I take, the road unfolds,
A tale of dreams, yet to be told.

The winding ways, both rough and sweet,
In silence deep, my heart does beat.
A journey wild, where few have been,
A dance with fate, a sight unseen.

With every turn, new wonders bloom,
In every heart, there's room to roam.
I find the strength in every fear,
The path less traveled draws me near.

I seek the stars that guide my way,
In fields of gold, I'll choose to play.
Uncharted lands where courage gleams,
Awake my heart, fulfill my dreams.

Beyond the Borders of Comfort

In shadows cast, I feel the call,
To venture forth beyond the wall.
A world awaits, both bright and vast,
With every breath, I break the cast.

The trembling heart, it learns to soar,
Past safety's gate, to seek for more.
Each step I dare, the thrill ignites,
A blaze of courage in the nights.

What lies beyond the comfort's net?
A tapestry of dreams unmet.
I'll chase the sun, the storm, the sea,
In search of all I long to be.

With open arms, I face the gale,
No longer bound by fear's frail veil.
The challenge calls, I hear it clear,
Beyond the borders, I persevere.

Fragments of Play in a Stiff Design

In corners neat, where shadows hide,
I find the spark of joy inside.
With whispered laughs and playful cheer,
A world unfolds, drawing me near.

The structure firm, yet veins of light,
Awake the dreams that take to flight.
Amidst the lines, all rigid, strong,
I weave my dreams, where I belong.

The rigid paths, they twist and bend,
In playful hearts, the rules can end.
With laughter bright, I break the mold,
In fragments free, my soul is bold.

So here I stand, a child at play,
In moments caught, I find my way.
A dance of colors, wild and free,
In each design, my spirit's key.

The Call of Untamed Ventures

A voice that stirs beneath the stars,
It whispers soft through space and scars.
Adventure waits beyond the door,
The wild unknown, I can't ignore.

With heart aglow, I chase the dawn,
To lands where few have ever drawn.
The rush of wind, the scent of pine,
In untamed ventures, I shall shine.

Each path I take fuels passion's fire,
The call is strong, my spirit higher.
I long to dance with fate's embrace,
In wild places, I'll find my grace.

So let me roam, let me explore,
To heed the call, forevermore.
In every step, my heart shall sing,
The joy of life, a wild offering.

Unshackled Horizons

Beyond the bounds of yesterday,
Dreams take flight on wings of hope.
Sky painted with shades of possibility,
We embrace the vastness, we elope.

Freedom whispers in the breeze,
Carving paths in unknown ways.
With hearts as our guiding keys,
We chase the dawn through endless days.

Thoughts untethered, spirits bold,
Navigating seas of uncharted fate.
Inspiration blooms, stories unfold,
The world awaits, inviting us to create.

Together we stand, hand in hand,
With courage to overcome the fears.
We journey forth through this uncharted land,
In pursuit of dreams across the years.

The Break of Dawn in Dusk's Embrace

In twilight's hush, the stars ignite,
A canvas painted, dark meets the light.
Whispers of night, secrets unfold,
As dawn creeps softly, bold and gold.

The world holds its breath in silence deep,
While shadows linger, secrets they keep.
Colors emerge with the rising sun,
A new day's promise has just begun.

Moments of magic, fleeting yet true,
Every heartbeat feels fresh and new.
The dance of light across the skies,
In dusk's embrace, a world will rise.

With every dawn, another chance,
To write our stories, to sing, to dance.
In every cycle, life finds its way,
From dusk to dawn, we greet the day.

Adventures Beyond the Schedule

In the folds of time, we wander free,
Chasing moments yet to be.
Beyond the clock's relentless chase,
We find joy in every place.

Turns unplanned, roads diversely laid,
The thrill of chance, the joy it made.
Maps of dreams, not just the paths,
Unwritten tales in the aftermaths.

With laughter as our guiding star,
We venture boldly, near and far.
In each detour, a treasure lies,
A serendipitous surprise.

So let's embrace the unexpected,
In the unknown, we feel connected.
Adventure's call, a sweet refrain,
In every hour, freedom's gain.

The Lure of Unfamiliar Places

A distant land calls out my name,
With whispers of secrets, wild and untame.
Footsteps echo on untraveled ground,
In the beauty of new, we're spellbound.

Where the sun sets in hues unforeseen,
And ancient tales weave through the green.
Curiosity ignites a spark,
In every corner, a story to embark.

The air is thick with possibilities,
A tapestry of unfamiliarities.
Each street and view, a song to learn,
In the dance of travel, our spirits burn.

So let's wander where we don't belong,
In unknown places, we find our song.
With hearts wide open, we shall embrace,
The thrill of each new, unfamiliar space.

The Lightness of Choosing Differently

In the morning light, paths unfold,
A breeze of options, bright and bold.
Each choice a feather, light as air,
Whispers of freedom linger everywhere.

With each step taken, a door swings wide,
Past shadows of doubt, where dreams abide.
The heart dances freely, unbound by fear,
In the lightness of choosing, all futures are clear.

A Dance Between Structure and Spontaneity

Under the moon's glance, rhythms collide,
Choreographed steps, yet wild inside.
A structure of notes that gracefully sway,
While spontaneity whispers, come out and play.

In the hold of a moment, let loose the strings,
Fusion of order and chaos it brings.
With every swirl, creation takes flight,
Together they flourish, both day and night.

Colors Beyond the Familiar Palette

A canvas awaits, unmarked and wide,
With hues yet to find, shadows to guide.
Brush strokes of dreams in vivid array,
Awakening visions that beckon to stay.

Mixing emotions, igniting the view,
In layers of stories, the heart's vivid hue.
Beyond what we know, a spectrum to chase,
In colors uncharted, we find our place.

Stirring the Stagnation

In still waters, dreams begin to wane,
Ripples whisper softly, calling our name.
A gentle nudge, a spark to ignite,
To awaken the world from its tranquil night.

With every small shift, the currents rearrange,
Old habits melt away, inviting the strange.
Embrace the unknown, let the waves roll,
In stirring the stagnation, we find our soul.

The Alchemy of New Perspectives

In the mirror of the mind, we see,
Shifting shadows, thoughts run free.
Colors blend in a dance divine,
Each hue a truth, each spark a sign.

Open eyes to worlds unknown,
Seeds of wonder gently sown.
Change the lens, and you will find,
The treasure lies in a curious mind.

With every step, discover more,
Unlock the wisdom at the core.
In every glance, a story made,
In every choice, a path arrayed.

The Enchantment of Unplanned Journeys

A road unfolds beneath the sky,
Where dreams may wander, and spirits fly.
Maps forgotten, hearts take the lead,
In every moment, adventure freed.

Whispers call from distant lands,
With open hearts and willing hands.
Each detour holds a secret light,
Guiding souls through day and night.

Find beauty in the unforeseen,
In lively streets or fields of green.
Joy is found in every chance,
In unplanned steps, life's wild dance.

Wings of Uncharted Skies

With wings unfurled, we dare to dream,
Soar above the quiet stream.
The skies await, a canvas wide,
Where hopes and fears in freedom glide.

Stars awaken in the midnight hue,
Whispers of the bold and true.
In every flight, a story gleams,
Onward we chase our vivid dreams.

Each cloud a promise, each breeze a guide,
In unknown realms, our spirits ride.
Through azure halls, we chase the sun,
With every journey, we have begun.

Break the Chains of Monotony

In daily rhythms, life can stall,
Routine's grip, a heavy pall.
Yet whispers call from the unknown,
To break the chains that we have grown.

A dance of color, a burst of sound,
In every corner, magic found.
Shake the dust from weary feet,
Embrace the wild, embrace the sweet.

Step outside the well-worn path,
Let laughter guide, let courage wrack.
With every choice, let passions burn,
In freedom's song, let hearts return.

The Heart's Bold Leap

In shadows deep, a whisper calls,
A pulse ignites, where courage sprawls.
With trembling hands, the moment near,
The heart prepares to face the fear.

Above the doubt, a flight begins,
With every breath, the spirit wins.
The leap unfolds, a dance of trust,
From ash of doubt rises the dust.

Through winds of change, the heart takes flight,
Embracing risk, chasing the light.
In every fall, a lesson learned,\nA fire born from passion burned.

With open arms to chance and fate,
The heart dives in, it won't be late.
For life's true joy is found in leaps,
In bold, wild dreams, the heart still keeps.

Seizing the Chances

The clock ticks on, the moments fly,
With every beat, a chance to try.
The world unfolds, its canvas wide,
Paint your dreams, let passion guide.

Step forth in faith, leave doubt behind,
In every choice, a treasure find.
Embrace the risk, let fear dissolve,
In this fierce fire, your heart evolves.

A path unknown, yet brightly lit,
With every turn, the spark will fit.
Seize the day with open eyes,
Transform your life, let courage rise.

For chances come like fleeting trains,
Ride every wave, embrace the gains.
In every heartbeat, life's adventure,
Seizing chances, your soul's true venture.

A Journey Beyond the Familiar

The road ahead, a winding path,
With every step, new tales to grasp.
Beyond the walls that once confined,
A world awaits, where dreams unwind.

Through valleys low and mountains high,
In search of wonders, we shall fly.
Each heartbeat sings a brand new song,
In every moment, we belong.

The stars above, a guiding light,
In unfamiliar, we find our might.
With every breath, horizons change,
A vivid life, no longer strange.

Embrace the unknown with open hands,
For in the journey, life expands.
Beyond the familiar, we explore,
New paths ignite our souls to soar.

Shaking Off the Dust of Predictability

In days routine, where patterns lay,
Life's clock ticks softly, shadows play.
Yet deep within, a spark remains,
To break the chains of mundane strains.

With every dawn, the chance to break,
To shake the dust in every wake.
Beyond the norm, a wild embrace,
Discover beauty in chaos' trace.

Each step we take, a chance to grow,
In freshened air, the river flows.
The unexpected lights the way,
From rigid roles, we find our sway.

So step on forth, ignite the flame,
Fetch the adventure, lose the shame.
For life's a canvas, bright and bold,
In shaking dust, our dreams unfold.

Chasing Shadows of Intuition

In the dusk where whispers blend,
Shadows dance, their messages send.
With every turn, the heart does race,
Following dreams, we find our place.

Secrets weave through twilight air,
A gentle pull, a silent dare.
Listen close, the truth reveals,
Within our depths, the spirit heals.

Guided by a soft inner light,
We trace the path through the night.
Moments fleeting, yet so embrace,
In every shadow, a hidden grace.

The journey calls, with no regret,
Each step taken, we won't forget.
Chasing shadows, bold and true,
Intuition leads, our spirits renew.

The Call of the Untamed Soul

In wild meadows, spirits soar,
Echoes of freedom, forevermore.
Whispers of nature, fierce and bright,
Awaken the heart to the call of the light.

The mountains rise, proud and tall,
Inviting the brave to heed the call.
In every breeze, a song is spun,
The untamed soul, forever young.

Through tangled woods and open skies,
The wild spirit learns to rise.
With every heartbeat, live the dream,
Flow with the river, dance with the stream.

Let passion guide, let courage flow,
To the rhythm of life, let us go.
Boundless horizons on this quest,
The call of the untamed, our souls find rest.

Sailing Beyond the Safe Harbors

Set the sails, the winds await,
Beyond the shores, we contemplate.
In the blue, adventure calls,
In every wave, the spirit enthralls.

Stars above, our guiding light,
Navigating through the endless night.
Fearless hearts with dreams to chase,
In vast oceans, we find our place.

With every swell, horizons shift,
In unknown waters, our spirits lift.
Boundaries fade, the self expands,
Together we journey, hand in hand.

Leaving comfort, ready to roam,
Sailing forth to find our home.
Beyond the safe harbors, we rise,
In the depths, our true self lies.

Fragments of an Unwritten Saga

Pages blank, a tale untold,
In every moment, we're brave and bold.
Ink of dreams, ready to flow,
Writing stories only we know.

Each heart beats a word sublime,
In the rhythm, we find our time.
Fragments linger, whispers stray,
Creating a path for the light of day.

With every breath, a vision grows,
In silence speaks what the heart knows.
A tapestry woven with threads divine,
We craft our fate, each sign a line.

Embrace the journey, don't look back,
In every fragment, fill the lack.
An unwritten saga, we'll embark,
With every step, we leave our mark.

Reveling in the Unexpected

A sudden storm, clouds intertwine,
Laughter echoes, a twist divine.
Whispers of joy, wild and free,
In every surprise, there's magic to see.

Umbrellas bloom, colors bright,
Dancing raindrops in soft twilight.
Every moment spins, a thrilling ride,
In life's surprises, we take great pride.

New paths appear, where shadows lay,
Adventures beckon, come what may.
With open hearts, the world unfolds,
A tapestry woven in threads of gold.

Celebrate the twist, embrace the stray,
In the unexpected, we find our way.
Let laughter ring, let spirits soar,
In the dance of life, there's always more.

The Freedom of a Whimsical Heart

Butterflies flutter, painting skies,
A fable written where wonder lies.
Giggles ripple through morning dew,
The world spins brightly, vibrant and new.

Chasing dreams on a fanciful breeze,
Every moment must aim to please.
With laughter as fuel and kindness as art,
The freedom blooms from a whimsical heart.

Bubbles of joy float all around,
In puddles of color, true bliss is found.
As stars giggle in the midnight glow,
A whimsical heart knows how to flow.

Every laugh opens a brand new door,
A dance through the chaos, always explore.
In the realm of magic, let's play our part,
For life is a journey that starts with the heart.

Navigating the Seas of Change

Waves crash softly, tides roll in,
Change is the anchor where we begin.
Set sail on dreams, let the winds guide,
In the heart of the storm, we find our stride.

Maps drawn in sand will shift with time,
The rhythm of life, a perfect rhyme.
With every rise, and in every fall,
Navigating change, we answer the call.

Stars light the way through nights so dim,
With courage strong, we learn to swim.
Each wave a lesson, each tide a friend,
In the seas of change, we blend and mend.

Embrace the current, let go of fear,
In the dance of change, we reappear.
With hearts as our compass, we sail afar,
And discover the beauty in who we are.

The Serenade of Unwritten Chapters

Pages blank, stories yet to weave,
Every breath a spark, a chance to believe.
Ink flows slowly, with dreams in tow,
In unwritten chapters, our hearts will glow.

Dancing shadows under soft-lit skies,
Whispers of hopes, where the future lies.
Each moment a note in a melody sweet,
In the symphony of life, we find our beat.

The quill dances lightly, stirring the air,
In each blank page, possibilities flare.
With every heartbeat, stories unfold,
The serenade breathes warmth, even when cold.

Embrace the unknown, let courage start,
For every unwritten chapter is a work of art.
In the journey of living, let your story flow,
In the essence of writing, together we grow.

Sculpting a Life Anew

In the silence, I carve my dreams,
Molding clay with gentle hands.
Each breath whispers new beginnings,
A masterpiece slowly stands.

Shadows linger, but they fade,
As sunlight warms the softest edges.
With every touch, I find my way,
Creating paths, breaking ledges.

The chisels echo deeper truths,
As I chip away the past.
A sculpture formed from every bruise,
In the journey, I find hope cast.

Now I stand, proud and free,
A life reborn in splendor bright.
With each new shape, I learn to see,
The beauty born from endless light.

Wading into the Wild Unknown

Step by step, the path unfolds,
Through tangled roots and whispered trees.
Adventures wrap like stories told,
In echoes carried by the breeze.

Curiosity ignites my heart,
With every leap, I find new ground.
In wilderness, I play my part,
Among the wonders yet unbound.

The moonlit night calls out my name,
Stars above like watchful eyes.
Each moment sparks a wild flame,
Guiding me toward the skies.

I wade deeper into the night,
Finding solace in the unknown.
With courage bold, I seek the light,
In every step, I'm not alone.

A Thousand Adventures Await

Beyond horizons, dreams take flight,
Where mountains meet the endless sea.
In every dawn, a spark ignites,
A thousand adventures call to me.

With open arms, I chase the sun,
To valleys new and skies so wide.
The world is vast, our hearts just one,
In every moment, we abide.

Beneath the stars, our stories weave,
Through laughter, tears, and endless play.
In every chapter, we believe,
That life is rich, come what may.

I gather tales from every shore,
A tapestry of memories made.
In every heartbeat, I'll explore,
A thousand paths, forever laid.

Embracing Life's Twists and Turns

Winding roads, they lead us on,
Through joy and sorrow, laughter, pain.
In every twist, a lesson drawn,
Life's dance, a beautiful refrain.

With every stumble, I find grace,
Rising up to greet the day.
In life's embrace, I find my place,
Learning, growing, come what may.

The seasons shift, a constant show,
Winter's chill gives way to bloom.
With open arms, I learn to flow,
Finding strength in every room.

So here I stand, with heart so true,
Embracing all that life has spun.
In every turn, I start anew,
With faith that every race is won.

A Breath of the Uncharted

In twilight's glow, a call to roam,
Where whispers lead to lands unknown.
With every step, a chance to grow,
A breath of air, where wild thoughts flow.

Amidst the trees, the shadows dance,
The heart leaps forth, embracing chance.
In valleys deep, where rivers wind,
New wonders wait for those inclined.

The stars above, a map of dreams,
A tapestry of whispered themes.
In silence deep, adventures spark,
A path unfolds beneath the dark.

So take a step, let courage lead,
For in the wild, we plant the seed.
A breath of freedom, untamed and free,
The uncharted beckons, come and see.

Beyond the Familiar Path

The road we know, a winding thread,
Yet beckons more, where none have tread.
A timid heart may hesitate,
But boldness calls to tempt our fate.

With every turn, a lesson learned,
In fields of gold, bright fires burned.
From hills that rise, to valleys low,
Beyond the familiar, we find our flow.

The sun dips low, with colors grand,
While shadows stretch across the land.
Each step a risk, each choice a chance,
A dance of fate, a daring glance.

So wander far, with spirit bold,
Stories await, yet to be told.
Beyond the familiar, let us thrive,
In the dance of life, we come alive.

The Art of Wandering Minds

In restless thoughts, ideas drift,
A canvas bright, with dreams to lift.
The mind, a traveler, freely roams,
In realms of wonder, it calls us home.

With every question, new paths arise,
In the garden of thought, imagination flies.
Like rivers flowing, ideas entwine,
The art of wandering, a gift divine.

Through labyrinths of dreams, we seek,
In whispers soft, the answers speak.
Where logic fades and magic flows,
The heart ignites, the spirit grows.

So let us wander, let us explore,
In the realm of ideas, we'll ever soar.
For in the art of mind's embrace,
We find our truth, we find our place.

Echoes of Unpredictable Skies

The storm rolls in, a wild surprise,
With thunder's roar, the lightning flies.
The heavens clash, a symphony's might,
Echoes of moments, both dark and bright.

Beneath the clouds, the world stands still,
The heart beats fast, with nature's thrill.
The rain pours down, a cleansing tide,
In unpredictable skies, dreams abide.

When sun breaks through, in radiant hues,
New light awakens the morning views.
With every dawn, a chance to rise,
In echoes of hope, we reach for the skies.

So let the winds of change embrace,
The beauty found in every trace.
For in the dance of storms and light,
We find our strength, we find our flight.

Chaos in the Calm

Within the stillness, storms arise,
Whispers of thunder, a muted surprise.
Waves crash softly against the shore,
Peace in the chaos, forevermore.

Nature dances, a waltz so wild,
In every heartbeat, the tempest smiled.
Calm's facade, a flickering light,
Life's little battles, hidden from sight.

Balance is fleeting, an endless chase,
Embrace the discord, find your place.
In the uproar, find calm's embrace,
Chaos and peace, a delicate space.

The Spark of Spontaneous Journeys

Footsteps lead to paths unknown,
Every corner holds a tone.
With a grin and heart set free,
Adventure calls, just wait and see.

Maps of dreams, inked with delight,
Wanderlust ignites the night.
No reservations, just an open mind,
In the thrill of the chase, treasures we find.

Every wrong turn, a story to share,
With every moment, a breath of flair.
Embrace the chaos, ride the wave,
For spontaneous journeys, the bold shall crave.

Unraveled Threads of the Daily Weave

Life's tapestry frays and pulls,
Yet beauty lingers, in fragile lull.
Colors blend in the morning light,
Threads of laughter, shadows of night.

Moments slip through the fingers of time,
Every heartbeat, a subtle rhyme.
Woven stories, in silence they hum,
Unraveled threads that lead us home.

In the mundane, the magic hides,
Find the patterns where joy resides.
For every weave, a tale to tell,
In life's fabric, we weave so well.

Serendipity's Gentle Hand

Fate's soft whispers guide the way,
Beneath the stars, where dreams may play.
Unexpected moments, like dew on grass,
Glimmers of fortune, they come to pass.

In laughter shared with strangers anew,
Serendipity dances, always true.
A chance encounter, a spark of glee,
The universe smiles, wild and free.

In the rhythm of life, let go of plans,
Trust in the magic of chance's hands.
For in the uncharted, wonders exist,
Serendipity calls, you must persist.

The Leap into Chaos

In shadows deep, we gather round,
The pulse of fear, a trembling sound.
With hearts aflame, we take one step,
And let the wild winds guide our prep.

The world a swirl of colors bright,
Each choice a spark igniting night.
We dive headfirst, abandon all,
As chaos whispers, we heed the call.

Unraveled threads, a tapestry torn,
In chaos born, our dreams are sworn.
Through every fall, we find our grace,
Embracing fate, we dare to race.

With laughter loud, we'll greet the storm,
In every twist, a chance to transform.
Together we leap, hand in hand,
Into the chaos, united we stand.

An Invitation to the Unknown

Open the door, hear the soft chime,
An echoing call from a place beyond time.
With every heartbeat, a path unfurls,
An adventure awaits, through unknown worlds.

The sky ignites with colors anew,
Whispers of stories in the morning dew.
Each step we take, a daring chance,
To waltz with fate in a cosmic dance.

Leave behind what you think is true,
Embrace the mystery, let it ensue.
For in the shadows, the light will gleam,
An invitation to dare and dream.

So gather your courage, take a deep breath,
In the unknown lies life, not death.
Set sail for horizons yet unseen,
In the heart of the void, we are keen.

Sunlit Paths of Divergence

Under the sun, we wander wide,
On divergent paths, our hopes collide.
With every step, a choice we make,
Each trail we take, a chance to awake.

The golden rays illuminate the way,
Branches reaching out, come what may.
Voices call from paths unseen,
To the right or left, where to glean?

In the dance of light, we lose our fears,
Chasing dreams through joy and tears.
With every twist, a tale unfolds,
Stories of courage, brave and bold.

So walk with me, take my hand,
Through sunlit paths across the land.
For in this journey, together we find,
The beauty of choices, entwined.

The Breakneck Sprint from Certainty

Caught in the snare of the known and safe,
We break the chains, begin the chase.
With hearts that race and visions clear,
We sprint from certainty, shedding fear.

The ground blurs fast beneath our feet,
Each stride a roar, a wild heartbeat.
As doubts dissolve in the wake of speed,
We find our strength, we plant the seed.

With every heartbeat, a whisper calls,
To leap from safety, to brave the falls.
In the frantic dash, we seek the fire,
To set our souls alight with desire.

So let us run with wild delight,
Beyond the shadows, into the light.
For in the breakneck sprint we dare,
To embrace the unknown, to breathe the air.

Breaking the Chains of Monotony

In the shadows where routine hides,
We seek a spark, where freedom bides.
Each tick of time, a heavy weight,
We long to break this silent fate.

With every dawn, a chance to rise,
To shatter walls, to touch the skies.
We dance beneath the unfolding light,
And cast aside the dreary night.

The chains that bind, we'll come to know,
Are only fables of the slow.
With courage bold, our spirits soar,
Together we can seek out more.

So let us sing of winds so free,
And find a world that dares to be.
For in our hearts, the fire remains,
To break the endless chains of pains.

The Dance of Unsung Days

In the quiet, colors blend,
Each moment lives, yet few attend.
A touch of grace, a laugh, a sigh,
In unseen rhythms, we flutter by.

With small delights, the hours sway,
The dance of life in soft array.
A whispered breeze, a fleeting glance,
In simple joys, we find our chance.

Though mundane paths seem cold and gray,
The unsung days demand their play.
Through gentle steps, our hearts align,
In every breath, the stars entwine.

So let us twirl in sacred space,
Embrace the wondrous, find our grace.
For in the dance of passing time,
Beauty lingers, pure and prime.

Whispers of Spontaneity

A sudden spark, a call to roam,
To wander far from hearth and home.
In fleeting moments, joy ignites,
As whispers beckon, soft as nights.

The unplanned path, a siren's song,
Invites our hearts where we belong.
With open minds and daring souls,
We chase the sun, while freedom tolls.

Each twist and turn, a tale unfolds,
In vivid hues of stories told.
With every step, the world's alive,
In spontaneity, we thrive.

So let us listen to the breeze,
Embrace the moments, flow with ease.
For life in whispers, bright and clear,
Reveals its magic, drawing near.

Untamed Journeys

Beneath the vast, uncharted skies,
Adventure calls, our spirits rise.
With every step on land unknown,
Our hearts written in the wind, have grown.

We travel paths where few have tread,
With dreams unfurling, no fears to shed.
In every corner, beauty wakes,
In mountains high and wildest lakes.

The road ahead, an open door,
To find the tales that life has stored.
Each twist is wild, each turn divine,
To journey far is to redefine.

So let us roam, let wanderlust lead,
For in the wild, our hearts are freed.
Untamed and bold, we find our way,
In every dawn, a brand new day.

The Pulse of Wild Curiosity

In the heart of the forest deep,
Where secrets and shadows creep,
Whispers call to the brave and bold,
Stories of wonders eager to unfold.

With every footstep, a new path shines,
Colors burst in vibrant lines,
Questions dance on the edge of night,
Yearning minds reach for the light.

Through tangled vines, surprises bloom,
Casting away the weight of gloom,
Nature's riddles beckon near,
Embracing the thrill, banishing fear.

In the pulse of wild, a spark ignites,
Fueling dreams on starry nights,
Curiosity, a flame that grows,
Leading us where adventure flows.

Unbound Roads Await

The horizon stretches, wide and clear,
Each winding turn draws us near,
Open skies hold our restless hopes,
Unbound roads teach us to cope.

Every mile reveals more grace,
New encounters in every place,
Footprints on trails unknown,
With every journey, we have grown.

The whispers of paths yet untaken,
Fuel our souls, unshaken,
Maps of dreams guide our way,
Chasing sunsets, we dare to stay.

Together, we sail on plotted charts,
Each direction a flash in our hearts,
The thrill of the ride, a sweet embrace,
Unbound roads, our endless space.

The Flicker of Unfenced Dreams

In the garden of wishes, they swirl and gleam,
A tapestry woven from every dream,
Flickering softly in twilight's glow,
Unfenced, they wander, daring to grow.

With hearts unchained, they dance and play,
Painting the sky in shades of clay,
Imagination takes flight on wings,
A symphony born of countless strings.

Through the meadows of thought, they roam,
Finding their way, they make a home,
Catching the winds of the wild and free,
Flickering softly, their spirit's glee.

Each dream a spark that braves the night,
Igniting the dark with hopes so bright,
Together they weave a tale so grand,
The flicker of dreams, hand in hand.

Serendipity's Gentle Touch

In the quiet moments, fate takes flight,
Unseen magic dances in the light,
Chance encounters, a sweet embrace,
Serendipity smiles, leaving a trace.

A whispered secret on the breeze,
Guiding us toward new discoveries,
Paths collide in the softest way,
Gently weaving night into day.

Here lies beauty in the small and rare,
A lover's glance, a tender care,
Life's unexpected, a cherished gift,
Serendipity's hands give hearts a lift.

With every heartbeat, new tales begin,
In the softness of fate, we find our kin,
Embracing the moments life bestows,
Serendipity's touch forever grows.

Journeying Without a Map

With each step, the path unwinds,
A dance of stars, where fate entwines.
The heart beats loud, a guiding light,
In shadows deep, we take our flight.

Winds whisper tales of distant lands,
Of dreams unfurling in gentle hands.
Through forests thick and mountains tall,
We wander boldly, ready to fall.

Every turn hides a story yet told,
The warmth of sun in the evening cold.
Through valleys wide and rivers deep,
We journey on, while the world sleeps.

In the silence, we find our way,
With every moment, unfolding day.
Without a map, we carve our fate,
Together bound, it's never too late.

The Fire of Rebirth in Still Waters

In still waters, sparks ignite,
A whisper soft, setting hearts alight.
From ashes grey, new life shall rise,
Through silent depths, hope never dies.

Reflections dance on a glassy place,
Where shadows fade, and light finds grace.
The fire burns with a healing glow,
In tranquil moments, the spirit flows.

Each drop a promise, a chance renewed,
In mirrored depths, find strength imbued.
A tranquil heart, awakening deep,
As waters cradle the dreams we keep.

From stillness surge the flames we crave,
In quiet battles, we learn to be brave.
With every ripple, a story is spun,
For in rebirth, our souls are one.

Echoes of Unseen Possibilities

In shadows cast by fading light,
Whispers call from the edge of night.
Unknown paths stretch far and wide,
Through echoes soft, our hopes collide.

Dreams take flight on wings of sound,
In silence rich, new worlds abound.
What could be lies just beyond,
In every heart, a poetic bond.

As stars align, we feel the pull,
Fractured moments becoming whole.
Through unseen doors, we dare explore,
In echoes sweet, we seek for more.

With every breath, new visions rise,
The canvas of life, vast as the skies.
And in the spaces, we come to see,
The beauty in all that might just be.

Glimpses of Unfettered Joy

In laughter bright, the shadows flee,
A spark ignites, wild and free.
With open hearts, we dance and sing,
Embracing all that life can bring.

Through fields of gold, we chase the sun,
In fleeting moments, we become one.
With every smile, the world unfolds,
As secrets of joy, together, we hold.

In every glance, a story shared,
A tapestry of love declared.
Through trials faced, we find our way,
In bursts of laughter, come what may.

For joy, unbound, is ours to claim,
In whispers sweet, we stake our name.
Together soaring, hand in hand,
In glimpses bright, we understand.

The Unexpected Symphony

Notes dance in the air, soft and light,
A harmony found in the still of night.
Whispers of laughter, hidden refrains,
Music unplayed flows through our veins.

A sudden crescendo, a burst of sound,
Each heartbeat syncing, lost and found.
In the quiet corners, melodies bloom,
Unexpected symphony fills the room.

With every surprise, a new chord strikes,
Echoes of joy that the heart likes.
An open window, a gentle breeze,
In this sweet chaos, we find our peace.

The world stops turning, just for a while,
We sway to the rhythm, lost in the smile.
In shadows and light, our spirits are free,
Creating a symphony, just you and me.

Mosaic of Moments Unplanned

Fragments of time, scattered and bright,
Each tiny piece holds its own light.
Interwoven tales, both bitter and sweet,
Life's grand mosaic, joyous and fleet.

A sunrise unexpected, colors collide,
In laughter and love, our hearts coincide.
Stolen glances, a spark in the air,
Uncharted moments, beyond compare.

Every heartbeat, a new shade appears,
A tapestry woven from hopes and fears.
In the chaos, a beauty unveiled,
Through unplanned journeys, our spirits have sailed.

We paint with joy, we sketch with our tears,
This mosaic of moments transcends the years.
In the canvas of life, we find our true stand,
Creating a story, hand in hand.

Escaping the Clock's Embrace

Tick-tock whispers weigh on the mind,
Chasing the hours, we feel confined.
A breath of freedom, a moment to spare,
In the rush of time, we seek to repair.

Loose strands of seconds, drifting away,
In shadows of dusk, we long to stay.
A fleeting twilight, a small escape,
In the dance of the stars, our spirits reshape.

Watch the clock fade, let worries disperse,
In the stillness we find, a universe.
From moment to moment, we choose to be free,
Escaping the clock, just you and me.

Time may shackle, but we hold the key,
In fleeting moments, we find our glee.
With every tick that we defy,
Our laughter and love paint the sky.

Breathing in Unscripted Air

Inhale the wild, the untamed, the free,
Each breath tells a story, calls out to thee.
The unscripted path, uncharted and wide,
In moments of silence, we learn to abide.

Wind in the trees, an unspoken rhyme,
Every exhale whispers, defying time.
With hearts wide open, we savor the day,
Breathing in magic, come what may.

Colors of life splash in the breeze,
No need for a script, just be at ease.
In the dance of the now, let your spirit soar,
Breathing in unscripted, forevermore.

Let go of the weight, take flight with a care,
In every heartbeat, we find the rare.
In the rhythm of living, our souls ignite,
Breathing in uncharted, hearts are alight.

Shattering the Glass of Repetition

Within the echo of the mundane,
A crack breaks free, a whispered change.
Routine like glass, too thin to last,
Shards beneath our feet, a path to rearrange.

Every tick of time, a chance to leap,
Into unknown realms, where dreams entwine.
We gather fragments, the past we keep,
A shattered mirror reflects the divine.

In chaos lies a beauty unbound,
A dance of freedom, a glorious mess.
With each new dawn, horizons surround,
We rise from whispers, and boldly profess.

No longer trapped in the cycle's snare,
We burst forth with laughter, alive and bold.
The glass of repetition, a story we share,
In shattered remnants, treasures unfold.

Portraits of the Unrestrained Heart

In colors bright, the heart reveals,
A canvas splashed with dreams and fears.
With bold strokes drawn, the truth it steals,
Each portrait tells of joy and tears.

The wildness flows from every vein,
No boundaries hold the passion tight.
With every heartbeat, with every strain,
Unrestrained love ignites the night.

Brushes dance in the golden light,
Creating visions, vibrant and clear.
In every layer, a joyful fight,
Unveiling what we hold most dear.

These portraits sing of souls set free,
In every hue, a tale unfolds.
An unrestrained heart's true melody,
In vivid colors, its story told.

The Adventure of Unfurling

Like a bud that breaks from winter's hold,
The heart unfolds beneath the sun.
Each petal whispers secrets bold,
In the dance of life, we come undone.

With every breath, a journey starts,
Unfurling dreams from hidden places.
A tapestry we weave with hearts,
Through shadowed trails and bright embraces.

The wind, it carries tales of flight,
As we spread wide, our spirits soar.
In the warm embrace of golden light,
We find the courage to explore.

Each unfolding moment, rich and rare,
An adventure woven through the song.
In the depths of love, we dare to care,
Together, unfurling, where we belong.

Shifting Sands on Stagnant Shores

Where the tide pulls back, concealed below,
The grains of time begin to shift.
A world in motion, a rhythmic flow,
In stagnant spaces, a silent gift.

Each grain reflects a life once lived,
With tales of struggle, joy, and strife.
They dance with whispers, secrets to give,
In the shifting sands lies the pulse of life.

The echoes of ages in every sweep,
A landscape forged by the passage of days.
Though shores may seem still, they hold what they keep,
In every wave, a memory stays.

So let the sands remind the shore,
That even in stillness, change will arrive.
In shifting cycles, life's essence is bore,
A dance of time, where we all strive.

Milton Keynes UK
Ingram Content Group UK Ltd.
UKHW022006091024
449514UK00007B/63

9 789916 884027